I want to be a thatcher man

JANICE NIBBS

CP

THE CHOIR PRESS

First published in the United Kingdom in 2022 by

The Choir Press

ISBN 978-1-78963-307-8 Hardback

ISBN 978-1-78963-308-5 Paperback

ISBN 978-1-78963-309-2 eBook

Illustrated by R. Vanterpool

This book is dedicated to future generations of Virgin Islanders who would like to understand what life was like in the early 1900's

Introduction

In times past, especially in the country-side areas of the Virgin Islands among farmers and the older generations, it was not unusual that these persons who "worked the land" often lived in homes that were quite small. The generation of the early 1900s were most likely the children of former slaves. Neither they nor their children who followed had been formally educated. Their homes were often made of materials that were readily available. While wood might certainly be used for the sides, building materials included dried vegetation such as tree branches and grass. Sometimes, a form of claylike substance that was made of limestone was used to hold carefully cut branches together to make the sides of a home. These latter homes were called wattle and daub houses.

Though most often it was the roofs that were made of grass, it was not unusual that a home was made entirely of these materials carefully woven together around a wooden "frame" to create a secure home that would protect those who lived there from the weather outside – whether it be heat, cold, rain or wind. The floors inside the homes were often bare earth. The yards around the homes also consisted of bare earth this was always swept clean. Just as homes today must be expertly built and maintained, this was also true for these "thatched houses;" that were commonly called "trash houses." The men of the village who were responsible for building and maintaining these homes were called "trashers."

As a small boy, Dennis enjoyed the time when the thatcher men came each year to thatch the home in which he lived with his parent and siblings. It was exciting to hear the men who were working on the inside of the roof shouting "Coming **up** to you-u-u. Take Slack, Take Slack." to the men who were working on the outside of the house or on the roof. They shouted this as they pushed a long wooden needle from inside the house, through the grass, to the outside. As the men on the outside returned the needle through the grass, they too shouted to the men on the inside. "Coming **down** to you-u-u-u! Take slack, take slack." This allowed them to know exactly where to stand to receive the needle when it came through and how much wis remained on the other side, to be pulled through.

Dennis looked forward to thatching day, as his uncle had promised, he would be able to help with the thatching process even more this year. He would be ten years old. Perhaps he would be allowed to help cut the grass that was used by the thatchers. He might also begin to learn other skills that he needed in order to become a thatcher man!

As his family prepared for the time when the men would come, Dennis' uncle began to teach him some of what he needed to know. He had him sharpen a machete that would be used to cut the grass. His uncle explained "The same tool can be used to cut sugar cane." There were two types of grass that were used to thatch houses. This depended on where on the island the home was located. Bull grass, was used in the Doty area and beyond. This grass grew to at least three feet tall. In the Great Mountain area, the guinea grass is used, this grass could grow as high as six feet. Uncle Benn explained that he preferred to use the guinea grass because it produced a taller stalk, and fewer lengths of it were needed to cover the height of the house, that is, to reach from the ground to the roof. Uncle Benn, who was a little over six feet tall, also explained that he preferred to make taller houses, because he could stand, rather than have to bend as he worked on the inside of the house.

Uncle Benn also showed Dennis exactly when the grass was ready to be cut. The grass would need to be just about to "arrow," that is, to develop the shoots from which the seeds would grow. If the grass was cut after it had arrowed, it would be necessary to discard too many dry blades of grass. For this reason, more grass would be needed to accomplish the thatching task. He also showed him how to tie the grass into small bundles. This would enable each thatcher man to have a supply of bundled grass on the inside, as well as on the outside of the house as they worked.

BUNDLES OF
GUINEA GRASS

Dennis knew that building a home was no simple task. There were many skills that he would need to learn if he wanted to be a successful thatcher man, he knew that it would take time. Afterall, he reminded himself, he was still quite young. He resolved that, once he had learned all that was needed, he would continue to build very small homes as a means of sharpening his skills. He wanted to be the best thatcher man in his community.

On the day he was to work alongside the men cutting the grass, Dennis woke earlier than usual, he wanted to finish his chores and be ready to go with Uncle Benn. He shifted the goats so they could have fresh food on which to feed for the day. He went to the well, and brought home several buckets of water. He went to collect the milk that was needed by his mother from Miss Phene. When he got there she was not ready. Her children had been late getting out of bed for the day, and she scolded them while he waited. His chores therefore took a bit longer than usual; so, his uncle had left without him. This was okay, because Dennis knew just where to find Uncle Benn. He would be over in the grass piece in the "hollow" close to where Cousin Elton lived.

When he got to the site, the men were already hard at work. Some were cutting the grass in rows. Others were arranging the cut grass into small bundles. Dennis easily found his uncle among the men. He was ready to begin the tasks his uncle would give him to do.

"Good Morning, Uncle Benn. Ah reach." said Dennis.

"Good." replied Uncle Benn. Then he continued . . .

"Now I can take a break as I teach you what to do.

"See these grass, notice that they are just about to arrow. We need to work fast over the next week, or we are going to lose a lot of our best grass. Remember we have many homes to repair and one new one to build."

"You need to cut the grass close to the root, so the trashers can have enough stems to work with." Uncle Ben continued.

Dennis listened attentively to the instructions his uncle was giving him.

Once he understood the instructions from his uncle, Dennis started by working slowly. He did not want to make any mistakes. It was not long before he found he was able to keep up with the other men. Uncle Benn noticed his progress, and suggested he take a short break. Dennis was pleased with himself.

After the break, he learned how to tie bundles. He learned what wis to use to tie them.

"See Dennis . . . we tie the bundles with pudding wis, or cat claw wis; but we can also use guard wis. We also use the same wis to thatch the house. By doing this, we make one trip to the forest for all that we need," said Uncle Benn.

6

Uncle Benn also took Dennis into the forest to show him how to cut the wis. Holding up a piece in his hand, Uncle Benn said, "See Dennis, we only cut wis in this size. We look for the ones in the size that we need; and only cut those. Someone else can use the other sizes. We must always think of others when we take an action. If we cut what we do not need, we will be wasting; and willful waste makes woeful want."

He showed him what wood to use. Wood from the birch tree is used to make the frame for the house. This is the preferred wood because it grows straight and is easy to handle, is dense in structure and is durable. When gathering wood to make anything always cut them on a dark night. The plants are not as full of sap and will not be so easily attacked by insects.

Dennis and Uncle Benn worked with the men for several days in order to prepare materials for thatching the homes.

On thatching day, Dennis' mother told him that she would get one of the other children to do his morning chores. In exchange, he would have to do their evening chores.

Dennis' home was one of those that was thatched on the sides, as well as on the roof. The thatcher men had selected a nice hot-sun day to do their work. They arrived early, and started to remove the old trash. As they worked they seemed to be speaking in a language that Dennis would need to learn. They carefully checked the frame of the house for any rotting timbers, just in case these would need to be replaced. Four to five upright posts were placed evenly apart.

They formed the frame of the house. A larger number of posts were placed horizontally (across). These sturdy pieces of wood formed the house frame. The horizontal posts were doubled so that the grass could be placed between them and attached to the frame posts. All the wood used to make the house was from the local birch wood.

FRAMEWORK OF A THRASH HOUSE

COCONUT BRANCH

BUNDLES OF GUINEA GRASS

There were small bundles of grass laid out all around the house on the outside as well as on the inside. Soon they would begin the part of the job that Dennis had been looking forward to with the most excitement. . . . that of actually thatching the house! It was an intricate task.

To accomplish the thatching process, the man on the outside grabbed as much grass as he could hold between his thumb and forefinger and packed this between two cross posts.

Using a long wooden needle that they had made of birch wood. He then made a loop, using a piece of wis around the grass. The loop was pulled tight as the man pushed the grass next to the bundle that had been placed before. He then passed the needle around the two cross posts and pulled the loop tight. To finish the process, he passed the wis around the frame post.

Then he passed the needle between the two bundles to the man on the inside of the house. It was then that that the man on the outside shouted "Coming <u>in</u> to you-u-u-u!' as he watched the sewing wis disappearing he instructed, 'Take slack. Take slack.' Grabbing the needle, the man on the inside repeated the process. He sewed his bundle of grass to the cross post and the frame posts, making sure that they were secure with the outside. He immediately passed the needle back to the man on the outside as he shouted, "Coming **out** to you-u-u! Take Slack. Take Slack.

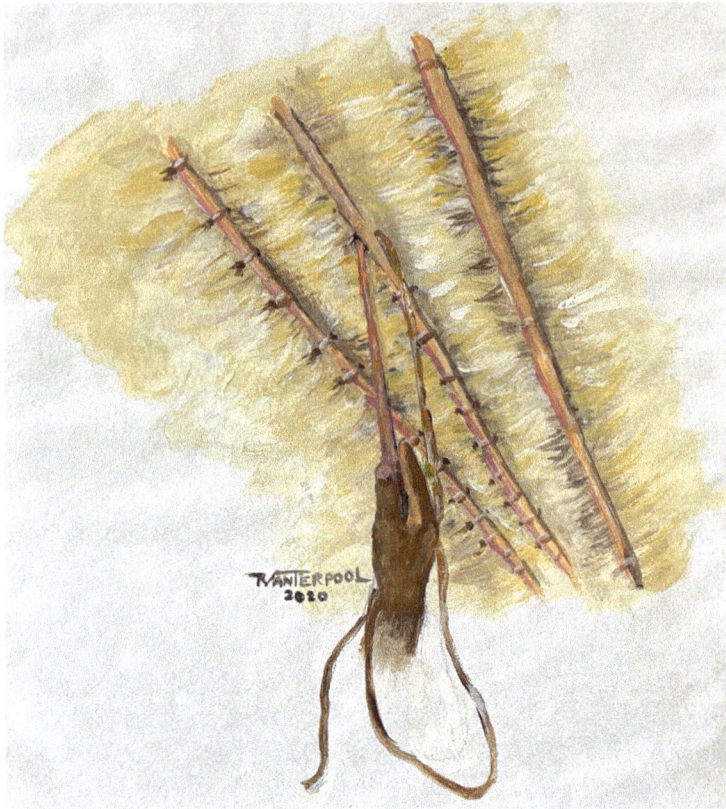

There was a total of about eight men. Two working each of the four sides of the house. They worked in pairs – one on the outside of the house, and one on the inside. Each pair of men started their work at the bottom or foundation of the house.

After observing the process for a while, Dennis was sure he could accomplish the task however complex it seemed. He watched closely as his Uncle Benn, working on the walls from inside the house, scrambled to take hold of the needle carefully attach his bundle of grass. He then shouted 'Coming out to you-u-u-u. Take slack, take slack," as he sent the needle back to his partner on the outside.

Sometimes, he would let Dennis pull the needle as it was pushed inside. He would allow Denis to sew a bundle in place then he would check the tightness of the wis before sending the needle back out. Each time this would happen Dennis felt a sense of pride his stitches were getting better and tighter. Soon he would be able to make them on his own

Because each bundle of grass was between three and six feet tall; once the third row was finished, the walls were high enough; and it was time to prepare for thatching the roof.

The house consisted of two long sides and two short sides. The roof was the same shape the men called this a "hip" roof. The roof was framed in the same manner as the sides of the house, with beams running both horizontally and vertically. In addition to the grass that was used for thatching the roof, coconut branches were placed directly on the beams of the roof in order to give the ceiling the appearance of a relatively smooth finish. Dennis found the thatching of the roof challenging; particularly since it

FRAMEWORK OF A THRASH HOUSE

was difficult to see where one bundle of grass started and ended. For this reason, it was necessary to depend on the shout each thatcher man in order to guess where the needle would appear when it was pushed to the inside or outside of the roof.

Making sure that the roof, the walls and the ridge of the roof showed a smooth finish also presented their own challenges. You needed to make sure that the edges were carefully sealed by bending the loose ends over and sewing them into a smooth tight finish. No wind or water must be able to get through.

Dennis worked hard alongside his uncle throughout the day. By the time the house was complete, he felt that he was almost ready to be a thatcher man himself. There were just a few areas he had yet to perfect. His sewing was not as neat, his edges needed a lot of work, and his bundles of grass as watertight as work done by Uncle Benn and other experienced thatchers. He was confident though, that if he continued to practice, he would be able to work with the best thatchers next time they were working in his village. Dennis took advantage of every opportunity he could to work on his skills.

By the time he was fifteen years, Dennis was considered one of the best thatchers in his village. In addition to framing out houses, cutting and bundling grass and thatching homes, he could also make the needles and identify and harvest the best quality of wis, grass and birch that were so important to making a well thatched home. His dream had become a reality. He had built himself a career from which he could make money. Dennis had become a thatcher man!

About the author

Janice is a native Virgin Islander who grew up on the brink of change between the traditional way of life and the social change to a prosperous economy. She always had a fascination with the old way of life. All the things she was told she was too small to do; go to the ghut to wash, go to the well, go on the bar fishing. She longed for these experiences not seeing them as drudgery but as something exciting. Today Janice is a retired librarian who realized that not much was recorded about life in these islands. She decided before the information completely disappeared she would record some information for future generations of Virgin Islands.

Series introduction

After slavery was abolished life for virgin Islanders changed. By 1841 most of the planters had left, the ex-slaves were left basically in control of the islands. They bought the estates as they came up for sale. Everyday life was a matter of survival. Being far from the other British West Indian colonies and with the seat of government being in Antigua money allocated for improvements took a long time to reach them. Their everyday survival depended on subsistence farming, fishing, charcoal burning and trade with their neighbors in the Virgin Islands of the United States.

Careers for young people depended on them being apprenticed to someone experienced in a specific skill so they could learn a trade. Often parents selected the skill they wanted for their child but in this series of books entitled the ***Traditional career series*** I am giving the young people the opportunity to select the skill they would like to have.